SUPERCARS

JAGUAR

Faith Woodland

www.av2books.com

Step 1
Go to **www.av2books.com**

Step 2
Enter this unique code
OUAGEZAP3

Step 3
Explore your interactive eBook!

AV2 is optimized for use on any device

Your interactive eBook comes with...

Contents
Browse a live contents page to easily navigate through resources

Audio
Listen to sections of the book read aloud

Videos
Watch informative video clips

Weblinks
Gain additional information for research

Slideshows
View images and captions

Try This!
Complete activities and hands-on experiments

Key Words
Study vocabulary, and complete a matching word activity

Quizzes
Test your knowledge

Share
Share titles within your Learning Management System (LMS) or Library Circulation System

Citation
Create bibliographical references following the Chicago Manual of Style

This title is part of our AV2 digital subscription

1-Year K–5 Subscription
ISBN 978-1-7911-3320-7

Access hundreds of AV2 titles with our digital subscription.
Sign up for a FREE trial at **www.av2books.com/trial**

SUPERCARS

JAGUAR

CONTENTS

JAG

UAR

JAGUAR SUPERCARS

Supercars are made with the most powerful engines. These cars are **luxurious**. They are built with the latest designs and technology.

The Jaguar car company is one of the greatest sports car and supercars manufacturers in the world. It is known for its stunning style and powerful products. Jaguars are winners on the racetrack. They are the pride of their owners.

Jaguar sold more than **100,000** vehicles in **2020**.

The most expensive Jaguar ever sold was a **1955 D-type**. It sold for more than **$21.7 million**.

WILLIAM LYONS

William Lyons and William Walmsley were two young men with big ideas. They started the Swallow **Sidecar** Company in 1922. The company designed and built sidecars for motorcycles.

Walmsley left the Swallow Sidecar Company in 1934. The same year, Lyons decided to use the company's **aerodynamic** design ideas to create cars. The company's breakthrough came in 1935, when the SS Jaguar car was released. Ten years later, Lyons changed the name of the company to Jaguar Cars Limited.

The Coventry Transport Museum, in Coventry, England, has a Jaguar Heritage Gallery. In the gallery, several historical vehicles showcase the history of Jaguar.

MAP OF THE UNITED KINGDOM

The Swallow Sidecar Company began in Blackpool, England. It moved to Coventry in 1928.

World Map

Scotland

United Kingdom

Northern Ireland

Ireland

Jaguar Production Plant, Castle Bromwich, England

Jaguar Headquarters, Coventry, England

Jaguar Production Plant, Solihull, England

Wales

England

Atlantic Ocean

N
W
E
S

SCALE
0
100 miles
100 kilometers

LEGEND

- Key Location
- United Kingdom
- Land
- Water

THE ROARING JAGUAR

The SS Jaguar sported a logo composed of a double *S* inside a hexagon. The hexagon had a bird tail and wings. After the Swallow Sidecar Company was renamed, its logo was changed to represent a silver leaping jaguar. The company also introduced a second logo showing a roaring jaguar. The roaring jaguar logo now appears on all Jaguar cars.

Until 2005, Jaguar cars had a three-dimensional leaping jaguar on their hoods.

JAGUAR LOGO

The jaguar represents strength and speed.

The silver color symbolizes **elegance** and modernity.

The red background represents passion for driving.

JAGUAR THROUGH HISTORY

William Lyons created fast, beautiful vehicles. Today, Jaguar continues his legacy by producing powerful and elegant sports cars.

William Lyons and William Walmsley start the Swallow Sidecar Company.

1922

1948

1951

The XK120 is launched. This is the first car using Jaguar's oval grille.

Jaguar's C-type wins the **24 Hours of Le Mans** race.

1961

Jaguar's E-type is launched. The E-type is regarded by many as one of the most beautiful sports cars ever made.

2008

Jaguar is bought by the Indian company Tata Motors.

2020

Jaguar unveils its new race car, the I-TYPE 5.

FAMOUS JAGUARS

Jaguars are among the most glamorous cars ever made. They have been featured in well-known films. For instance, M, one of the main characters in the James Bond movies, can be seen riding a Jaguar XJ-L in the movie *Skyfall*. Many villains drive Jaguars in other movies of the James Bond franchise, including *Die Another Day* and *Spectre*.

The Jaguar C-X75 was part of a chase scene in *Spectre*.

Actor Harrison Ford, soccer player David Beckham, and TV star Simon Cowell all own Jaguars. Queen Elizabeth II is also a fan of Jaguar. Over time, she has been seen driving or riding in different Jaguar **models**, such as the S-type and the X-type.

Simon Cowell drives a 1965 E-type Eagle Speedster.

In 2018, Prince Harry and Meghan Markle drove a Jaguar to their wedding reception.

David Beckham became a Jaguar brand ambassador in 2014.

AT THE RACES

Jaguar has a long history of racing in many different categories. The XK120 model won many races, including the Silverstone Production Car Race in 1949 and different rallies in 1950 and 1951. Between the 1950s and 1990s, Jaguar won the 24 Hours of Le Mans race seven times. Jaguar also won the Daytona race in 1988 and 1990.

Jaguar's racing division is now called Jaguar Racing. Jaguar Racing currently only competes in **Formula E**. However, the Jaguar team also raced in **Formula 1 (F1)** between 2000 and 2004.

Mitch Evans has been racing with Jaguar since the company made its Formula E debut in 2016.

At the time of its introduction, the XK120 broke the record for the fastest production car in the world.

Jaguar ended the Formula E **2017/2018 season** with **119 points**, its best result to date.

During a practice run for the 1954 Le Mans race, the Jaguar D-type reached the record speed of almost 173 miles (278 kilometers) per hour.

Jaguar Racing scored its **first Formula E win** at the Rome ePrix of **2019**.

Drivers Eddie Irvine and Johnny Herbert raced with Jaguar during its first F1 season in 2000.

HOW IT'S MADE

Most Jaguar cars are built in England by robots and skilled craftspeople in two state-of-the-art plants located in Castle Bromwich and Solihull. The high-tech robots in each plant are used to assemble the vehicles. Craftspeople then customize each order.

The Solihull and Castle Bromwich plants are open to visitors. People can explore both facilities and learn more about Jaguar's production process.

The Castle Bromwich factory was used to build war airplanes in the late 1930s and 1940s.

The Solihull plant sits on a 300-acre (121-hectare) site.

Castle Bromwich has the **world's largest aluminum press** to create Jaguar's aerodynamic form.

627 robots work in the Jaguar plant of **Solihull.**

The F-pace model is produced in the Solihull plant.

In 2020, Castle Bromwich closed for a few months. This was because the COVID-19 pandemic caused a shortage of computer chips that were needed for vehicle production.

TODAY'S LINEUP

Jaguar has dazzled people with its design for nearly 100 years. The company continues to develop beautiful cars today. Customers can choose from many different models and customize their choice to their liking.

Here are some of the Jaguars on the road today.

Jaguar XE S

Engine: **P250 RWD Automatic**

Maximum Horsepower: **250**

0–60 mph (0–100 km/h): **6.7 seconds**

Starting Price: **$40,600**

Jaguar XF S

Engine: **P250 i4 Gas**

Maximum Horsepower: **246**

0–60 mph (0–100 km/h): **6.5 seconds**

Starting Price: **$44,000**

Jaguar I-pace S

Engine: **EV400**

Maximum Horsepower: **394**

0–60 mph (0–100 km/h): **4.5 seconds**

Starting Price: **$69,850**

Jaguar F-pace SVR

Engine: **P550 AWD Automatic**

Maximum Horsepower: **550**

0–60 mph (0–100 km/h): **3.8 seconds**

Starting Price: **$84,600**

Jaguar F-type R Coupé

Engine: **P575 V8 GAS AWD**

Maximum Horsepower: **575**

0–60 mph (0–100 km/h): **3.5 seconds**

Starting Price: **$103,200**

Jaguar XE SV Project 8

Engine: **Supercharged V8**

Maximum Horsepower: **600**

0–60 mph (0–100 km/h): **3.3 seconds**

Starting Price: **$188,500**

TOMORROW'S JAGUAR

Jaguar is investing many resources in the development of new technologies. The company plans to produce only electric cars by 2025.

The most recent Jaguar **concept car** is the Vision **Gran Turismo GT** SV. While Jaguar built a life-sized prototype, the Vision Gran Turismo GT SV is not a real car. Jaguar designers created it for a video game. In the game, the car is fully electric. It has a maximum horsepower of 1,877 and can reach a speed of 255 miles (410 km) per hour.

The first version of the Vision Gran Turismo GT SV was unveiled in 2019.

Some concept cars, such as the C-X75, never move to production.

The Jaguar C-X75 concept car was created to celebrate the 75-year history of Jaguar.

The I-pace concept car was first presented in 2016. It was the first electric car made by Jaguar.

JAGUAR QUIZ

1 Who started the Swallow Sidecar Company?

2 Who raced with Jaguar during its first F1 season?

3 When was the first Jaguar car built?

4 What was the first car to use Jaguar's oval grille?

5 What race did Jaguar win in 1951?

6 What company owns Jaguar now?

7 When was the I-pace concept car first presented?

8 What Jaguar model appeared in the movie *Spectre*?

9 How many robots are used at the Solihull plant?

10 Where is the F-pace model produced?

ANSWERS
1 William Lyons and William Walmsley
2 Eddie Irvine and Johnny Herbert
3 1935 **4** The XK120 **5** The Le Mans
6 Tata **7** In 2016
8 The C-X75 **9** 627
10 In the Solihull plant

KEY WORDS

24 Hours of Le Mans: the world's oldest active motorsport race, held in France since 1923

aerodynamic: having a shape that reduces drag created by air

concept car: car built to show off new technologies and designs

elegance: richness of beauty and style

Formula 1 (F1): the highest level of single-seat car racing

Formula E: single-seat car racing using electric cars

Gran Turismo GT: a car that seats two people

luxurious: pleasing, comfortable, and expensive

models: particular car designs made by a company

sidecar: a passenger seat attached to the side of a motorcycle

INDEX

Published by AV2
276 5th Avenue, Suite 704 #917
New York, NY 10001
Website: www.av2books.com

Library of Congress Cataloging-in-Publication Data

Names: Woodland, Faith, author.
Title: Jaguar / Faith Woodland.
Description: New York, NY : AV2, [2022] | Series: Supercars | Includes index. | Audience: Grades 2-3
Identifiers: LCCN 2021022175 (print) | LCCN 2021022176 (ebook) | ISBN 9781791138813 (library binding) | ISBN 9781791138820 (paperback) | ISBN 9781791138837 (ebook other)
Subjects: LCSH: Jaguar automobile--Juvenile literature. | Sports car racing--Juvenile literature.
Classification: LCC TL215.J3 W66 2022 (print) | LCC TL215.J3 (ebook) | DDC 629.222/2--dc23
LC record available at https://lccn.loc.gov/2021022175
LC ebook record available at https://lccn.loc.gov/2021022176

Printed in Guangzhou, China
1 2 3 4 5 6 7 8 9 0 25 24 23 22 21

072021
101120

Art Director: Terry Paulhus
Project Coordinator: Sara Cucini

Photo Credits
Every reasonable effort has been made to trace ownership and to obtain permission to reprint copyright material. The publisher would be pleased to have any errors or omissions brought to its attention so that they may be corrected in subsequent printings. AV2 acknowledges Getty Images, Alamy, and Shutterstock as its primary image suppliers for this title.